An introductory guide to
Inductive Bible Study (IBS)

NOTICE OF COPYRIGHT

The material in this workbook (other than Scripture references) is copyrighted—Register of Copyrights, USA.

Registration Number— TXu 1-571-065 (August 13, 2007)

Permission to copy and distribute this material needs to be obtained in writing.

Under no circumstance is any person allowed to charge fees for this workbook, or any of the material within it, unless expressly authorized in writing by the author. Under no circumstance is any person allowed to charge fees for this workbook, or any of the material within it, unless expressly authorized in writing by the author.

To obtain written permission or further information about the materials in this workbook, please contact the author, Howard (Trip) Kimball at the address below.

Living Word Study

Pastor Trip Kimball

Jacksonville Beach, FL 32250, USA

E-mail – info@word-strong.com

Scripture quotations are from the ESV® Bible (The Holy Bible, English Standard Version®), copyright © 2001 by Crossway, a publishing ministry of Good News Publishers. Used by permission. All rights reserved.

8th Revision (LWS) — updated October 2022

[ESV]

This 8th Revision was updated March 2023 and includes a guide for developing inductive study questions, along with an inductive study of the Book of Ruth.

Foreword

[*This is a revised and condensed version of a published workbook*] As featured on www.Word-Strong.com

The Inductive Bible Study (IBS) approach has been used for many years in many ministries

It is an effective and reliable approach to studying the Bible. It is objective and impartial to any scripture text, and provides an accurate study of God's Living Word—the Bible.

IBS can be described as applied hermeneutics or a text-based approach to exegesis—the text being the Scriptures.

Hermeneutics is the art and skill of using accepted rules of interpretation for understanding the Bible (from a Protestant and Evangelical perspective).

It is more than a systematic method—it is both dynamic and interactive.

Interactive because it involves the participant (student) with the Holy Spirit's guidance in the learning process.

Dynamic because it leads to the ongoing and transforming work of the Holy Spirit who gives understanding to your mind while working the truth into your life (the application step in IBS).

Living Word Study (LWS) is designed for both leaders and learners.

LWS is useful for anyone who would like to deepen his or her understanding of the truth found in God's written Word.

Structure and flexibility are built into the instruction of the LWS workbook. A person can apply the LWS process for an in-depth study, a survey-style study, a devotional study, or somewhere in between.

What makes IBS a reliable approach for studying the Bible?

IBS is not a mechanical method of study, but a mindset, an attitude of the heart.

The apostle John declares the Holy Spirit is our Teacher (1 John 2:27), echoing what the Lord Jesus told His disciples in John 14:26. The apostle Paul declares God's written Word is both inspired and able to equip any person for any ministry—

> All Scripture is breathed out by God and profitable for teaching, for reproof, for correction, and for training in righteousness, that the man of God may be complete, equipped for every good work. (2 Timothy 3:16-17)

The foundation of the Scripture and the guidance of the Holy Spirit is the basis for the Living Word Study workbooks and other developed studies.

This introductory guide is a fresh, simple, yet thorough introduction to studying God's Living Word using the Inductive Bible Study process.

I believe God's written Living Word is a sufficient foundation for both individual spiritual growth and for developing leaders who are thoroughly equipped for whatever work of ministry the Lord may call a person to do.

The instruction and guidelines in this workbook have been developed, tested, and proven fruitful in the lives of thousands of pastors and leaders for over 25 years in the US, the Philippines, Thailand, and several other places in the world.

I hope it will be a blessing to you in your study of God's Word so that you will be a blessing in whatever manner the Lord calls you to serve Him.

    By His grace,

[signature: TMP]

Trip Kimball / missionary-pastor, author-editor – Living Word Study

A Basic Introduction to Inductive Bible Study (IBS)

Inductive Bible Study Basics

Is Inductive Bible Study the only way to study the Bible?

Many good resources are available for studying the Bible. The goal of this study guide is to provide a simple, complete approach to studying God's Living Word. For simplicity's sake, let's consider two common study approaches—

Here is a simple, comparative look at two study approaches...

INDUCTIVE STUDY

- **Is objective and systematic—** leading to a thorough study of all Scripture

- **Discovers the details of the text—** by observing the words and phrases of the Scripture text

- **Investigates these details—** to fully understand the truth within a text

- **Examines the text—** so the truth is revealed by the Holy Spirit

- **Induces truth from the text—** the truth in the text stands out by reading, rereading, and study

DEDUCTIVE STUDY

- **Starts with a premise—** an idea believed to be true

- **Works to prove this idea—** by finding Scriptures to support this idea called proof texts

- **Assumes the idea is biblical—** because proof texts seem to prove it

- **Deduces a truth from the text—** attempts to prove idea is true

Introductory Guide to Inductive Bible Study

DEDUCTIVE STUDY: works to prove a conclusion believed to be true

> Ideas (premises) → Text (proofs) → truth?

- Deductive study is mainly used for topical teaching because it's focused on one specific topic or idea
- When the premise is true, it is a safe method. But if the premise is not true, then the resulting conclusion is also not true!
- Biblical truth needs to be studied within its context for an accurate understanding of the truth

A *false* premise, which is proven, results in false beliefs or false truth, which can also produce false teaching.

INDUCTIVE STUDY: draws conclusions from what is discovered in the text within its own context and the Bible as a whole

> Text (details) → Ideas (insight) → Truth!

- Premises or ideas about truth believed need to be the result of thorough reading and studying of the scripture text
- Carefully and accurately observe what is written in Scripture before drawing any conclusions about the truth within it

Inductive study enables you to learn *all* doctrinal topics and subjects within their context in the Bible.

The Basics of IBS

IBS helps a person discover the Truth in a Scripture Text through 3 basic steps:

1. Observation

The 1st step of IBS is a simple and thorough examination of the written words and phrases of the scripture text. It is the most important step in the process.

It sounds simple and is simple. But it is not to be ignored, nor done carelessly. It affects everything else that follows it.

A key element in observing a text well is to read the Bible text several times before you begin your study. This will help you see the truth in its own context.

2. Interpretation

The 2nd step is the process of studying to understand the meaning of the details (words and phrases) of what is observed in the scripture text.

There are valuable guidelines for doing this step, but it must be preceded by accurate and careful observation. Interpretation is often much simpler when observation is done well.

3. Application

The 3rd and final step is putting the understanding gained (in step 2) into practical life action. This step makes it possible for the truth to become real and useful in daily life. In a sense, it is a translation of the truth from words into action.

Two important questions help take our study from theory and concept into practical action— *What will I do?* and *How will I do it?*

The 3 Basic Steps of Inductive Bible Study

make it possible

...to move from knowledge

...to understanding

...to practicing the truth

IBS is not a mechanical method but a process that needs to be guided by the Holy Spirit

Inductive Bible Study Basics

Text Structure

It is important to have a good understanding of the structure of whatever book you study in the Bible

- It becomes a frame of reference to understand the truth discovered. This is the text structure.

- The text is the written Scripture, the Bible. Understanding it helps you see the context (see Luke 24:25-27; 44-45).

> When the context becomes more clear you gain insight into the details of the text

Seeing the text structure is much like working with a puzzle

- It is difficult to understand the importance of each piece unless you see how it fits into the whole picture. But you need all the pieces to see the whole picture.

- The pieces are all the details in the Scripture text—the words and phrases. The whole picture is the text structure itself.

Context

...the parts of Scripture that give it meaning

There are two kinds of context to consider

1. The immediate or textual context. This includes the surrounding (nearest) words, phrases, and verses of the word or phrase being studied
2. The general or whole context includes the larger parts of the text—even the Bible itself

the Text

...the way the text is written is its structural form

Begin with the Bible as a whole, from Genesis to Revelation. Within the Bible, there are 66 books, 39 in the Old Testament and 27 in the New Testament. The Bible and each of the 66 books are the general or whole context.

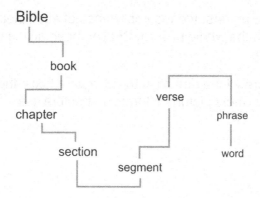

In the Addenda you'll find the text of John 13:1-5 (ESV) given to provide an example of how to study a Bible text using the IBS approach.

The text is already broken into small segments (groups of verses) to make it easier to apply our 3 steps of IBS—Observation, Interpretation, and Application. **Next, we'll look at the process of each step of IBS**

Step 1 — Observation

What does the text say?

What is actually written down as words and phrases within the Scripture text? What has God spoken through those who wrote it? This is what you need to ask yourself as you read and study God's Living Word.

Here are some simple, useful ways you can do this step of observation well—

- **Begin to study by reading and rereading the text**
- **As you read—make note of important words and phrases**
- **Have a notebook handy to write down important details you discover**
- **Ask key questions as you read and study through the Scripture text**
- **Be able to retell the story and put the truth of the text IYOW (In Your Own Words)**

Introductory Guide to Inductive Bible Study

Developing Observation Skills

Observation involves examining the details—the words and phrases—of the text in an objective, systematic, and accurate way.

How can you discover these details?

You need to know what to look for and how to see it. You need to ask the right questions for the correct answers.

Simple but important questions will help you discover these details accurately. These key questions help unlock the truth in the words and phrases of the text.

① Who?

② What?

③ Where?

④ When?

⑤ How?

> Observation is the first and most important step in the study process.
>
> Everything else rests on how well it is done.

Step 1 – Observation

Ask these 4 Key Questions as you read and observe the text—

"Who?"
This question refers to people

- Who are the people involved in the story (written text)? Not only the names of people but their identity.
- What does the text say about who they are? What are the people's roles and relationship to others involved? Who is speaking? Who is doing something?
- Take note of pronouns, both singular and plural, and ask— who does each pronoun represent? What do the impersonal pronouns connect to?

"What?"
This question refers to events and actions

- What happens in the story? What are the events taking place? What activities are going on? What are the people doing?
- Are they working, walking, praying, or doing something else? What are the people saying? What is spoken, taught or questioned?
- What are their actions? This might include meals, discussions, arguments, reactions, or expression of feelings (fear, anger, joy, etc.)

"Where?"
This question refers to Location or Places

- Where do events take place? Where are the places mentioned in the story (text)? What types of land or locations are mentioned in the text?
- Are there fields, mountains, or seas? Where are the people going or coming from? You may need a map (or atlas) to locate and discover names of place, cities, regions, or countries.

Introductory Guide to Inductive Bible Study

"When?"
This question refers to Time

- When did this story take place? What is said giving any idea of time or the historical time period? When does the story start? ...end?

- What is in the past, present, or future as expressed in the text? How long does it take from one event to another? Is there a progression of time taking place?

These 4 Key Questions are inter-related and work together in telling the story to help you discover relationships between each of the details...

- **People are involved in the various events and actions that happen**
    - The question "Who?" refers to people and is directly related to the question "What?" (events and actions)
- **Events take place at certain times and in certain places and usually involve people**
    - So, the questions "Where?" (location) and "When?" (time) are also related to the questions "Who?" and "What?"

As you observe and understand the interdependence of all the details observed—

- you begin to see the context of what you read and observe
- you begin the transition towards interpretation

4 Important elements to observe when studying narratives (stories)

Narratives include the books of the Pentateuch, Historical books, and the Gospels

1. **People**— *Whoever* is involved or mentioned by name or description within the story (text)

2. **Events and Actions**— *Whatever happens* or takes place within the story—including conversations, meals, and other common events or actions

3. **Places**— *Where* people are and events occur— geographical and physical locations or descriptions expressed in the text

4. **Time**— *When* events or actions take place in the text— chronological time, dates, seasons, timing, or sequence (progression)

Each of the four elements corresponds with the first 4 Key Questions

1. People— *Who?*
2. Events and Actions— *What?*
3. Places— *Where?*
4. Time— *When?*

Introductory Guide to Inductive Bible Study

Here is a fifth important Key Question to ask...

"How?"

This refers to the Way events and actions happen or take place

How is closely related to the question "what?" (events and actions) but also to the other questions— "Who?", "Where?", and "When?"

- How did the events happen? In what way did things happen?
- How did the actions take place? In what way are people doing things?
- How do the events and actions affect the people directly or indirectly?
- How do things change with circumstances, relationships, or within history (time), and where things take place?

"How?" is an important investigative question—a question that goes deeper in observation of a text than the first 4 Key Questions

It answers the question—

- How are the four basic elements of a narrative inter-related?
- How are they connected?
- In what ways are each of these four basic elements affected or influenced by the others?

"How?" is a transition question between the first 4 Key questions and the primary question of the 2nd step of IBS Interpretation ("Why?")

1. It describes the process of the story—how the story takes place.
2. It explains the inter-relationship of the four important elements—people, events and actions, places, and time.
3. "How?" is the *glue* of the context— When you see how the four elements are interrelated and affected by each other—then you can understand the context and go on to answer the question "Why?"

Step 1 – Observation

The Value of Story
How it all connects

Inductive Bible Study (IBS) is a systematic approach to Bible study, but should not be overly analytical. Jesus said, *"The words I speak to you are spirit, and they are life" (John 6:63c)*.

In a narrative (story), when you see the context more clearly and see how the people, events and actions, places, and time fit together as a whole, the story will come alive for you.

This enables you to enter into the story as an experiential observer rather than an objective bystander.

Here's why—

- When the truth comes alive it can be internalized and abide in you (John 15:7) and begin to transform your life.

- When the truth is understood, you should be able to put it into your own words (IYOW = in your own words).

- When you can share a story in your own words (IYOW), you can bring the same experiential sense of the story to others, so they can enter into the story in a similar way as you did.

- When you're familiar with the biblical stories you've studied and can relate them IYOW, you can connect your life story to God's story—the story of redemption throughout the Bible.

- Jesus did this with parables and situations (Matt 21:28-32; Luke 7:36-50), so you can also learn to link biblical stories to the life stories of others and their personal situations.

Telling a story well

People love stories anywhere you go in the world. People engage with stories easily. Their interest is captured and held when the story is told well.

People are further engaged in the story when given the opportunity to answer questions about details in the story. As people participate in a discussion of the story, the IBS approach through biblical storying becomes an effective way to share God's story of redemption, whether one-on-one or with a small group.

A simple guide for learning how to tell a story IYOW can be found in the Addenda. You can use the 5 Observation questions discussed earlier to engage people in discussion with the story.

Here are some sample IBS questions to ask—
1. Who seem to be the most important people in this story?
2. What are they doing and how are they involved with the story?
3. Where does all this take place?
4. When do these things happen?
5. How are the people connected to one another or are they?
6. Why do you think they react as they do?
7. What truth can be learned from this story and how could it be useful or valuable to you in your life?

As you become more familiar with a story by telling it many times IYOW, you'll learn how to tailor your questions to how people understand and engage with the story. The more you do it the better you'll get at it!

Remember, the original form of the Bible was oral *not* written. When the story and its truth is internalized in you, it goes with you wherever you go!

When you engage others in the story and they learn it, it will stay with them too.

Step 2 — Interpretation

"How can I understand what I have observed?"

The focus of the 2nd step of IBS is to look for spiritual insight and understanding. Again, this is not to be a mechanical or scientific process, but a study guided by the Holy Spirit.

There are 5 Basic Rules for helping interpret the Scripture—simple, general and useful for personal Bible study or for teaching and equipping leaders.

They are guidelines developed by scholars and theologians and accepted by the Protestant church worldwide.

The 5 Basic Rules for Interpretation:

1. **Study within the whole context**—this includes the surrounding words and verses up to the whole Bible, and the cultural-historical context.
2. **Interpret the Scripture literally**—not literalism, but finding the plain and simple meaning of what is written.
3. **Let Scripture interpret Scripture**—other Bible texts give insight and clarity to the text being studied.
4. **New Testament (NT) Scriptures help interpret the Old Testament (OT)**—since the NT is the fulfillment of the OT.
5. **What is obvious and clear (explicit) is more important than what could be true (implied)**—what is clearly stated should always be considered more important than what could be meant.

"How do I apply these rules?"

1. Prayer and guidance from the Holy Spirit are your starting point.
2. Rereading the text is still important in this 2nd step.
3. Other study references may give insight into the culture, history, and other contextual information.

Living Word Study — Introductory Guide to Inductive Bible Study

Developing Interpretation Skills

Interpretation is understanding the meaning of the details discovered by observing a scripture text

Examine your observations with the following three things in mind:

1. **Study with a fresh attitude—** read and study as if you've never read or studied the text before.

2. **Set aside previous ideas, teachings, and biases—** set aside what you or others think it means and work from the what you've observed by using the 5 Key Questions— "Who... What... Where... When... How?"

3. **Use the 5 Basic Rules of Interpretation called hermeneutics.** Hermeneutics are basic principles of interpretation—applied with both art and skill—to understand the meaning of a Bible text. IBS is one form of applied hermeneutics.

> Rereading the text, understanding the context, and accurate observation will do more to improve your interpretation skills than anything else

Step 2 — Interpretation

"Why?" is often answered by simple observation

- Accurate observation will help you understand why something takes place, or is said, or doesn't happen.

- When you answer the question "Why?" correctly, you will get an accurate explanation (interpretation) of the meaning and purpose of what you observed.

Answering the question "why?" requires discernment

Discernment sees beyond the obvious [see 1 Corinthian 2:10-14]

Here are 3 things needed for discernment:

1. Be guided by the Holy Spirit—see John 14:26; 1 John 2:27
2. Use the 5 Basic Rules of Interpretation (hermeneutics)
3. Use your own thinking and sound judgment

Examples:

See the following stories for illustrations of discerning the truth—

- Matthew 16:5-12— Jesus' disciples gain insight (discernment)

- Luke 7:36-50— Jesus, a Pharisee, and a sinful woman

- Luke 20:1-8— Jesus, Jewish leaders, and questions

- Luke 20:19-26— questions about taxes to trap Jesus

- Luke 24:13-35— opened eyes and burning hearts

So, how do we do this?
This is where the IBS study process deepens

- Hermeneutics is the art and skill of applying rules of interpretation—rules proved and accepted by theologians over several centuries.

- IBS is applied hermeneutics, also called exegesis—the critical (analytical) explanation or interpretation of a scripture text.

IBS is a personal, interactive process of studying the Bible

- Pray and ask the Holy Spirit for His guidance!

- When the Holy Spirit is actively involved in your study process, it will keep the IBS study process from becoming stiff and mechanical.

- It will become a dynamic and life-changing experience!

5 Basic Rules of Hermeneutics

1. Study the Scripture within Its Context
The surrounding words, their setting, and reference within the Bible

- Study the immediate and whole context of a scripture text—it helps clarify and confirm the truth in the text

    - This gives a better understanding of the details of the text and makes the truth stand out more plainly

    - Remember to read and study the Scripture text from the point of view of the author and the original hearers and readers

- Study the full context—including geography, along with the manners and customs of that historical time

    - Various reference books give insight into biblical culture and times

    - Commentaries may be useful for cultural insight, meanings of words, and cross-references, but are not divinely inspired writings

    - Do your own inductive study before looking to commentaries and other references

2. Look for the Plain and Simple Meaning

Understand how words are expressed as the writer intended

- Read and understand the Bible the same way you read other literature.
    - Rules of grammar and composition are the same as secular writings
- Look for the plain and simple meaning of the text, first
    - What is the obvious or plain meaning? What seems to be the natural meaning of the text? Don't read into the text what isn't there
    - Generally, what it says is what it means
- Look for words that express more than their simple definitions.
    - When words are used in a different way than their usual meaning, they are called figures of speech—they represent a different meaning than their normal use
    - How words are used is what gives them meaning

3. Let Scripture Interpret Scripture

The Spirit of Truth (the Holy Spirit) Reveals the Word of Truth

- The Scriptures are revealed and inspired by God (2 Tim 3:16)
    - The Scriptures are the written record of God revealing His truth to man, and through man (2 Peter 1:20-21)
    - The Scriptures will not conflict or contradict each other! What is true in one place is true in another (Numbers 23:19; Titus 1:2)
    - The written word of truth is trustworthy (Psalms 19:7; 119:138, 144)
- The immediate and whole context is an important priority
    - The immediate context is found within a section or chapter, the surrounding words, phrases, and verses—the whole context can extend from a whole book to the whole Bible
    - A concordance is helpful for finding parallel verses and cross-references.

4. New Testament Scriptures Help Interpret the Old

Doctrine and theology revealed in the NT is a replacement and fulfillment of what God revealed in the OT

- Jesus fulfilled the Law and the Prophets (the Old Covenant Scriptures and established the New Covenant (Matthew 5:17). This is especially important with doctrinal truths and theology

- The New Testament (Covenant) fulfills of the Old Covenant
    - Jesus fulfilled all the Law's requirements, and the teaching and prophecies of the prophets, in the Scriptures (Luke 24:25-27; 44-47)
    - The New Covenant is superior to the Old (Heb. 7:22; 8:6, 13; 9:15)

5. What is Obvious and Clear (explicit) is More Important than What Could Be True (implicit)

Don't go too far with your interpretation!

- Whatever is clearly stated and expressed is most important
    - Accurate observation is very important! It is always the most critical and important step in IBS. If you start off in the wrong direction, you're likely to keep going that way!

- What could or might be intended is less important
    - It can be tempting to look for an indirect meaning that may be suggested by someone else, but Rule #2 needs to be kept in mind

- What is clearly stated is more important than what could be meant
    - Keep the context in mind (Rules #1 and #3!) when studying a specific scripture

Step 3 — Application

"How should I respond?"

This is the question you need to answer for the truth to become real and active in your daily life. Answering these two primary questions will help make your application more specific.

The 1st question is— *What will I do?*

- What is a useful way to apply the truth in your daily life? How can you make abstract, conceptual biblical truth become a concrete reality?

- You can begin to do this by asking yourself more specific questions

    - Are there commands I need to obey? Is there a discipline I need to develop and keep? How can I learn from the example seen in the text being studied? How can I be a better example for others?

- Ask similar questions for promises to believe or exhortations to embrace

    - What kind of problems, situations, and sins do I need to avoid? These questions should lead you to see how to trust and follow the Lord more closely in your daily life.

The 2nd question is— *How will I do it?*

- How will you actually do (or not do) these things?

    - What are actual steps you will take? This is what makes an application work. Make a specific list of how you can start applying truth you come to understand.

- Consider when you will start to put these truths into action

    - If you don't work through this step, you simply gain more Bible knowledge, but only with good intention.

The Goal of Application:
Make it practical! Make it personal!

1. What do I need to do?
- Make abstract truth become concrete reality
- Put theological truth into practice

2. How will I do it?
- Applications need to be specific, personal, and practical

- **Your personal study should be worked into your own life first**
  - Application requires seeing the useful ways biblical truth can be put into action in daily life
- **Look for a key verse or word to anchor the application to the text**
  - This makes the application more specific
- **An application needs to be both simple and practical**
  - Applications should be made of a useful and important truth— something that can be done—an action taken, an attitude of heart, or perhaps something not done
- **Applications should flow from your inductive study of a text**
  - Usually, only 1 application is needed for each segment or verse depending on the type of text it is

---

The goal of application—apply the truth in a practical and personal way

- Most of the time—only one application is needed for each segment
- More than one application per segment may be needed when studying Epistles, some areas of Biblical Prophecy, and with the Gospels

Developing Application Skills

The Bible is clear about a person's responsibility to obey the truth once it is known and understood

- As you begin to understand the truth drawn out of the Bible through your inductive study, you need to apply it—put it into real-life action

Look up and review these references:
John 13:17, 14:15; 1 John 2:4-6; Matt 7:24; James 1:22-25

- Based on what is written in these texts, a person is not to be just a hearer, but a doer of the Word

- Application of the truth needs to be seen within the original context first for it to be sound and appropriate

How would the original hearers and readers apply this same truth?

- This is an issue of context—both historical and textual context—which helps with understanding the actual content (truth) of the Scripture

Once—you see how it would apply within its original context—the timeframe, geographical setting, and manners and culture

Then—you can begin to apply it within present day life—just remember these basic guidelines:

- Your personal study should be *worked into your own life first*

- Look for a *key verse or word* that anchors the application to the text

- An application needs to be both *simple and practical*

- Applications should flow from your inductive study of a text

Living Word Study — Introductory Guide to Inductive Bible Study

2 important questions need to be answered...

1. What will I do?
2. How will I do It?

Remember—

- thinking is not doing and verbs are action words
- the questions below help you see how to make applications

1. What will I do?

What action will you take now that you understand the truth?

1. Are there any commands to obey or exhortations to respond to?
2. Are there disciplines you need to develop or keep in your life?
3. Is there an example you need to follow or be setting?
4. Is there a promise for you to believe or trust God in?
5. Is there a sin you need to forsake, an error to correct, or a specific situation to avoid?

2. How will I do it?

In what way will you put this truth into action?

1. How will you make these changes or take certain actions?
2. What are the actual steps you can or need to take?
3. Why will you do this?
4. When will you begin to do this

Addenda

Here are some helpful study guides to put the
3 steps of IBS to work when studying a Scripture text

Addenda

Addenda

Quick Review of the Inductive Bible Study Process

Observation — 1st Step of IBS

5 Key Questions / 4 Elements

1. **Who** is involved and included?
   - People—individuals, groups, nations, etc. (notice pronouns!)

2. **What**'s happening?
   - Events and Actions

3. **Where** is it happening?
   - Places and Locations

4. **When** is it happening?
   - Time—time of day, chronological, sequential, historical, etc.

5. **How** is it all connected and happening?
   - Ways things take place / happen—descriptions, emotions, processes, customs and manners, the relationship of each element to one another.

Inductive Bible study draws conclusions—from what is discovered in Scripture within its own context and the Bible as a whole.

Text (details) ➔ **Ideas** (insight) ➔ **Truth!**

- Premises or ideas about truth ought to be from a thorough reading and studying of the Scripture text.

- Carefully and accurately observe what is written in Scripture before drawing any conclusions about the truth within it.

- An Inductive study enables you to learn *all* doctrinal topics and subjects within their context in the Bible.

Addenda

Interpretation — 2nd Step of IBS

5 Basic Rules

1. **Context**—The immediate and whole textual context, and cultural and historical elements of context
2. **The Plain and Simple Meaning**—Are words expressed in literal or figurative language?
3. **Scripture Interprets Scripture**—Consider the context and harmony of the Bible as a whole
4. **NT Helps Interpret OT**—Old Covenant Law fulfilled in New Covenant by Jesus
5. **What is Obvious takes Priority over Implied**—What is clearly and plainly intended and expressed is more important than what could be meant

Studying and Journaling

Remember, answering *why* requires mental and spiritual discernment (guided by the Holy Spirit) that leads us to gain insight.

Put yourself in the context of whatever you're reading— "see and hear" it from the writer's point of view—i.e. put yourself in the place of the disciples with Jesus.

As you read and study, make notes in your Bible and keep some note paper handy. This will be a reference for more detailed study and journaling.

Addenda

Application — 3rd Step of IBS

Putting Truth into Practical Action

- **Answer these 2 Important Questions**

1. *What* will you do?
    - Translate your understanding of the Scripture text into useful life-action
2. *How* will you do it?
    - What are specific ways or in what manner will the truth become useful and practical in your life?

Remember—thinking is not doing and verbs are action words.

- Turn abstract truth into concrete reality
- Put theological truth into practice
- Be specific, personal, and practical

Simple Outlining of the Scripture Text

1. Break the Scripture text into Segments
2. Group the Segments into Sections
3. Discover the Theme of the book

Simple Outlining helps with seeing the big picture and how specific details fit into the larger picture of a Section of Scripture.

Work segment by segment and verse by verse based on your outline.

Work observation by observation within each verse for more detailed study and journaling.

Addenda

LIVING WORD STUDY — IBS QUICK REVIEW ©2018 (revised 2021)

Observation — 1st Step of IBS

5 Key Questions / 4 Elements

1. **Who** is involved and included?
   - People—individuals, groups, nations, etc. (notice pronouns!)
2. **What's** happening?
   - Events and Actions
3. **Where** is it happening?
   - Places and Locations
4. **When** is it happening?
   - Time—time of day, chronological, sequential, historical, etc.
5. **How** is it all connected and happening?
   - Ways things take place / happen—descriptions, emotions, processes, customs and manners, relationship of each element to one another, etc.

Inductive study draws conclusions—from what is discovered in Scripture within its own context and the Bible as a whole.

Text (details) → Ideas (insight) → Truth!

- Premises or ideas about truth ought to be from a thorough reading and studying of the Scripture text
- Carefully and accurately observe what is written in Scripture before drawing any conclusions about the truth within it
- Inductive study enables you to learn all doctrinal topics and subjects within their context in the Bible.

Interpretation — 2nd Step of IBS

5 Basic Rules

1. **Context**—The immediate and whole textual context, and cultural and historical elements of context
2. **The Plain and Simple Meaning**—Are words expressed in literal or figurative language?
3. **Scripture Interprets Scripture**—Consider the context and harmony of the Bible as a whole
4. **NT Helps Interpret OT**—Old Covenant Law fulfilled in New Covenant by Jesus
5. **Obvious takes Priority over Implied**—What is clearly and plainly intended and expressed is more important than what could be meant

Studying and Journaling

Remember, answering "why" requires mental and spiritual discernment (guided by the Holy Spirit) that leads us to gain insight.

Put yourself in the context of whatever you're reading — "see and hear" it from the writer's point of view—i.e. put yourself in the place of the disciples with Jesus.

As you read and study, make notes in your Bible and keep some note paper handy. This will be a reference for more detailed study and journaling.

Application — 3rd Step of IBS

Putting Truth into Practical Action

- Answer these 2 Important Questions

1. *What will you do?*
   - Translate your understanding of the Scripture text into useful life-action
2. *How will you do it?*
   - What are specific ways or in what manner will the truth become useful and practical in your life?

Remember—thinking is not doing and verbs are action words.

- Turn abstract truth into concrete reality
- Put theological truth into practice
- Be specific, personal, and practical

Simple Outlining of the Scripture Text

1. Break the Scripture text into Segments
2. Group the Segments into Sections
3. Discover the Theme of the book

Simple Outlining helps with seeing the big picture and how specific details fit into the larger picture of a Section of Scripture.

Work segment by segment and verse by verse based on your outline.

Work observation by observation within each verse for more detailed study and journaling.

Addenda

Living Word Study Notebook
—a study journal—

The Living Word Study (LWS) Notebook is a simple way to study a Scripture text more completely in one handy notebook or as a devotional journal

Here are some helpful things to keep in mind—

- The LWS study journal helps make the inductive study process a written, systematic reference—a study tool for Bible study or a devotional journal

- The first and most important step is careful reading and rereading of the Bible text—mark the text for observations while reading and rereading

- Break the text studied into segments—segments are groups of verses with a similar event or action, people, conversation, or idea, etc.

- Study through each segment, look for one primary truth—discover what the Holy Spirit wants to reveal to you as your read and reread the text

- What stands out to you?

- Look for a key verse where the primary truth is anchored

- Use the actual wording of the Scripture text for your observation—the interpretation can be written out following the observation

- As you observe the primary truth of a segment, write it down and explain it IYOW—an explanation *in your own words*—that makes your study both personal and practical

- Add Scriptures that are helpful and necessary for understanding the text—including cross-references and parallel verses that help explain the primary truth of the text

- Determine how the primary text can be applied in real life—as you gain insight into a biblical truth, see how to put it into practice in daily life

Addenda

On the following page is an example of how a simple inductive study of the text of John 13:1-5 looks using the LWS study journal.

John 13:1-5 (ESV)

Segment 1 (vss 1-5)

1 Now before the Feast of the Passover, when Jesus knew that his hour had come to depart out of this world to the Father, having loved his own who were in the world, he loved them to the end. 2 During supper, when the devil had already put it into the heart of Judas Iscariot, Simon's son, to betray him, 3 Jesus, knowing that the Father had given all things into his hands, and that he had come from God and was going back to God, 4 rose from supper. He laid aside his outer garments, and taking a towel, tied it around his waist. 5 Then he poured water into a basin and began to wash the disciples' feet and to wipe them with the towel that was wrapped around him.

> A text of John 13:1-17 can be found later, followed by 3 pages of Observation, Interpretation, and Application study questions for a complete Inductive Bible Study of that section.

Addenda

Living Word Study Journal (Example)
a journal and notebook for Bible study

Text Segment— *John 1:1-5*   **Date**— *today*

Key verse— *vs 1*

Observation— *...having loved his own who were in the world, he loved them to the end.*

Primary Truth— *Jesus demonstrated His love in a sacrificial way*

Interpretation— *Jesus demonstrated His love to the disciples and people of Israel many times by showing them mercy, teaching that connected with them, praying for and healing them, and even befriending those who were marginalized by the Jewish leaders.*

The expression "loved them to the end," means He loved them to the... fullest extent. This is also expressed in the famous John 3:16 text– "God so loved the world...." We see this in His going to the cross as "the Lamb of God who takes away the sin of the world." (John 1:29)

The love of Jesus was shown in every aspect of His life, including Jesus washing the disciples' feet in this story, including Judas His betrayer.

Application— *Even as Jesus demonstrated His love for the disciples and the people of Israel (John 1:11), I also need to consider ways I can love others.*

I need to think about those I find it hard to love or express love towards. I need to consider the practical ways Jesus showed love to other people, as well as to the disciples.

I can love others in these ways...

    (this is where you give actual and practical ways to show love to specific people)

I will love others by... because...

    (here you can be specific about how you will love others—who they are, why this expresses love to them, and when you will do this)

Addenda

Definition of Terms

Segment
A Segment is a group of verses related by a similar thought or idea

This unifying idea separates it from the verses before and after it. A Segment may contain two to several verses, all having a common thought or subject.

An example of a Segment would be John 1:29-34—

This group of verses can be considered a Segment because of the following:

- It begins with "The next day..." which gives us a time reference
- It is telling of John the Baptist's first testimony about Jesus
- This testimony about Jesus is further explained in verses 31-34
- The following verse (35) is on the "next day" where two disciples begin following Jesus

Section
A section has many segments related to each other

- A section may be part of a chapter, a whole chapter, or cover more than one chapter.
- The segments are related or grouped together because of similar subjects or events, just as verses are that make up a segment.

Main Theme
Every book in the Bible has a main theme

- The main theme is a general, prevailing idea expressing the *content* of the book as a whole.
- It can be expressed in a single word or phrase (3-5 words) and as a summary of the book's purpose and content.
- For example, the main theme of Genesis could be stated as—
  Beginnings or *In the Beginning*.

Addenda

Making a Simple Outline

Outlining is a way to see the text structure in a brief form
1. Outlining helps you study in a systematic, step-by-step process
2. Outlining helps you see the whole context
3. Outlining helps in working with the immediate context

First, break the text into segments
After reading and rereading the whole text you're studying, whether a book or a chapter, group verses into segments—with similar people, events or truths

- **Each segment should have at least one key verse that can be seen as an anchor for the main focus of the segment**

    ◦ This key verse stands out as a point of reference for the segment

    ◦ It may have key (very important) words or a key phrase

    ◦ It may be whatever verse expresses the whole or general idea of a particular segment

Once— you identify all the parts of the text structure
- the words and phrases (the details of the text)
- the segments (groups of verses with common details or truth)
- and sections (groups of segments)
- and the main theme (the general message of the book)

Then— you can begin writing out the outline

Addenda

You can outline any book of the Bible with this 3-step process:
1. Break the text of the book into segments
2. Group the segments into sections
3. Discover the main theme of the book

- Simple outlining helps you remember people, events, and truth within chapters of a book

- Familiarity with people, events, and truths within a scripture text helps you remember where it is located in the Bible

- As you read and reread the text, it becomes natural to remember things within their context and where it is in the Bible

---

3 Important Elements of a Simple Outline

1. **State the Main Theme of the book**—in a few words, describe the general message or focus of the book

2. **Start with the first Section**—note the chapter and verses where each Section begins and ends—also give a brief description of the content

3. **Outline segments within each Section**—give the verse references where each segment begins and ends, with a brief description

(write out the outline like the example that follows)

Addenda

Example of a Simple Outline

(using the book of Genesis)

Theme: Beginnings or In the Beginning

Outline:
I. Creation— Gen. 1:1–2:25 (section #1)

    A. In the Beginning— Chap 1:1-2 9 (segment 1 of section #1)

    B. 7 Days of Creation— Chap 1:3–2:3 (segment 2 of section #1)

    C. Man and Woman— Chap 2:4-25 (segment 3 of section #1)

II. The Fall of Humanity— Gen. 3:1–4:16 (section #2)

    A. Temptation and Sin— Chap 3:1-7 (segment 1 of section #2)

    B. Consequences of Sin— Chap 3:8-24 (segment 2 of section #2)

    C. Extension of Sin— Chap 4:1-16 (segment 3 of section #2)

III. 2 Genealogies Gen. 4:17–5:32 (section #3)

(continue through the book of Genesis in this way)

John 13:1-17 (segment outline)

Theme: Servant-leadership

Outline:

1. The Confident Servant-Leader [Son of God]—vss 1-5 (key vs— 1)

2. The Servant-Leader's Example [Son of Man]—vss 6-11 (key vs— 8)

3. The Servant-Leader as Teacher [Messiah]—vss 12-17 (key vss— 14, 17)

Addenda

John 13:1-5 (ESV)

Segment 1 (vss 1-5)
1 Now before the Feast of the Passover, when Jesus knew that his hour had come to depart out of this world to the Father, having loved his own who were in the world, he loved them to the end. 2 During supper, when the devil had already put it into the heart of Judas Iscariot, Simon's son, to betray him, 3 Jesus, knowing that the Father had given all things into his hands, and that he had come from God and was going back to God, 4 rose from supper. He laid aside his outer garments, and taking a towel, tied it around his waist. 5 Then he poured water into a basin and began to wash the disciples' feet and to wipe them with the towel that was wrapped around him.

Segment 2 (vss 6-11)
6 He came to Simon Peter, who said to him, "Lord, do you wash my feet?" 7 Jesus answered him, "What I am doing you do not understand now, but afterward you will understand." 8 Peter said to him, "You shall never wash my feet." Jesus answered him, "If I do not wash you, you have no share with me." 9 Simon Peter said to him, "Lord, not my feet only but also my hands and my head!" 10 Jesus said to him, "The one who has bathed does not need to wash, except for his feet, but is completely clean. And you are clean, but not every one of you." 11 For he knew who was to betray him; that was why he said, "Not all of you are clean."

Segment 3 (vss 12-17)
12 When he had washed their feet and put on his outer garments and resumed his place, he said to them, "Do you understand what I have done to you? 13 You call me Teacher and Lord, and you are right, for so I am. 14 If I then, your Lord and Teacher, have washed your feet, you also ought to wash one another's feet. 15 For I have given you an example, that you also should do just as I have done to you. 16 Truly, truly, I say to you, a servant is not greater than his master, nor is a messenger greater than the one who sent him. 17 If you know these things, blessed are you if you do them.

Addenda

Observation Study Questions

Here are some specific Observation questions related to John 13:1-17

Review these questions as you study this text—

1. What specific things did Jesus know in verses 1-3?
2. What specific actions did Jesus do in verses 4-5?
3. Who is involved or mentioned in this first segment (vss 1-5)?
4. What things are said or done, and by whom in vss 6-11?
5. What specific things does Jesus say in verses 6-11?
6. What does Jesus say and do in verses 12-17?
7. What specific command or exhortation is given (in vss 12-17)?
8. What promise is given with this exhortation?

Addenda

Interpretation Study Questions

Here are some Interpretation questions related to John 13:1-17

Review and answer these questions as you study this text—

1. What specific things did Jesus know in verses 1-3?

2. Why do you think the apostle John makes it clear what Jesus knew?

3. How is this related to what Jesus does in verses 4-5?

4. Why do you think Peter answers Jesus the way he does in verses 6, 8, and 9?

5. Why do you think Jesus answers Peter in the way He does in verses 7, 8 and 10?

6. Why was it hard for Peter and the disciples to understand why Jesus washed their feet?

7. What is the double picture of Jesus that we see in verses 2-5?

8. What picture of Jesus do we see in verses 12-17?

   a) How is it different than in verses 4-5?

9. Why are these pictures needed for the disciples (and us!) to understand what Jesus wanted to teach them in this story?

Addenda

Application Study Questions

Here are some specific Application questions related to John 13:1-17

Review these questions as you study this text and be specific, personal, and practical!

1. What are ways others have loved and served you?

2. How would you feel about someone of greater authority or position serving you in this way?

3. What are ways you have humbled yourself to serve others?

4. What are specific ways you are loving and serving others now? (practical and useful ways of serving others)

5. What application did Jesus want His disciples to make in verse 17?

6. How could this be applied today for us as believers?

7. How, as leaders of ministries?

8. In what ways can you be a servant-leader?

Developing Inductive Questions for Small Group Studies

Using the text of John 13:1-17 (NKJV)

Copyright – July 2006 / TK

Living Word Study for Small Groups

There are many ways of putting the Living Word Study (LWS) approach to studying the Bible into practical and fruitful use. An especially effective way is by using Inductive Questions (IQs) as a means of leading people through a Bible text. When doing this, you become more of a leader or facilitator of the study rather than a lecturer or teacher doing all the talking.

Leading a study this way provides an opportunity for people to discover the truth on their own. As they are directed through the text by using inductive questions, the Holy Spirit will reveal the truth to them personally.

The questions need to be developed and asked in a way that encourages both thought and discussion. For most people, it will take time to learn how to ask good questions and to ask them well. **Jesus** is our great example, of course, when it comes to asking good questions well.

This workbook is designed to help you *begin* learning how to do this. However, the learning process really *begins* when you *actually put this instruction into practice.* There are *no shortcuts.* It will require adequate preparation, a commitment to helping others discover the truth, and a willingness to learn from experience.

There are risks involved in teaching this way. You need to be willing to make mistakes and learn from them. It's all part of the *learning curve.* But it is well worth it. Especially when you experience the joy of watching people arrive at the moment of, "a-ha, *now* I understand!"

Examples of Small Group Studies

Small Group Bible Studies — for men, women, couples, or any other group of believers. It encourages interaction and discovery of the truth by all involved. Inductive questions help people stay on track and focused on the text rather than being sidetracked by opinions, misguided thoughts, or rabbit trails.

Discipleship — of an individual or within a small group. It can be used for young believers or even as a means of evangelism. It can be very useful for following up on crusades or personal evangelism in one-on-one relationships.

Leadership Development — within the church, in church planting, and even in para-church ministries. It can be a great way for interactive, yet directed instruction, that provides training and guidance for leaders. The level of depth in a study can be adjusted for different levels of maturity and experience.

Children and Youth Ministry — for all ages and all group sizes. Sunday School curriculum can be designed or enhanced to encourage observation and interaction using inductive questions. Youth ministry can become more dynamic and challenging for young people of all ages.

Chronological Bible Storying — another way to use inductive questions, but within an oral learning environment. Inductive questions are a great way to help people walk back through a Bible story and gain insight into the truth of the story. Inductive questions can lead to a much deeper understanding of the story's truth, as well. The questions may be prepared ahead of time or be spontaneous, or a combination of preparation and spontaneity, led by the Holy Spirit. It is a highly effective means of evangelizing, discipling, and training people in oral cultures and oral learning settings, those who prefer to learn by an oral teaching approach.

The following information and instructional guidelines should help explain and guide you through the process of developing Inductive Questions (IQs) to lead a Small Group Bible Study (SGBS). Inductive questions direct people into observing, interpreting, and applying God's Word, leading them into discovering the truth.

Developing Inductive Questions

Inductive Questions (IQs) *apply* **the inductive approach in leading others in their study of a Bible text.** These questions are based on a thorough inductive study of the text being studied, as with the Living Word Study (LWS). They can be effective for looking at a verse or a few verses, for devotional study. They are equally effective when studying through an entire book, individually, one-on-one, or in a small or large group.

IQ's can help a person accurately examine and investigate a text. These questions can *lead* people into a clear understanding of a text. They can *guide* people into *putting the truth* being learned into *life-action*. In this way, the three basic steps of inductive study — *observation, interpretation and application* — are applied for discovering truth within the Bible.

IQ's are valuable to anyone involved in leadership. Simply because, they are useful in leading people through a Bible study while modeling the process of how to study inductively. In this way, the leader becomes a model (example) not only in the learning process, but in how to lead others in a study. IQ's provide for a systematic and complete examination of a Bible text. This is especially effective in working with small group studies, discipling others and even for personal studies.

Think about how often Jesus used questions in the Gospels. He did so very effectively. He is our greatest teaching example for teaching and discipling others. He used them when speaking to great crowds, the twelve disciples, sometimes with only three of them.

Consider some examples

In Chap 16 of Matthew's gospel, Jesus uses questions to spur the disciples to remember two miracles that were intended to teach them about trusting God. Then with another question, He leads them to understand what He was originally speaking to them about (see Matt 16:5-12). Later in Chap 16 (vss 13-15), when they arrive at another place, He uses questions that result in Peter's confession of faith about whom they believe Jesus to be.

In the Gospel of Luke 10:25-37, Jesus utilizes questions to lead a seeking "expert in the law" to answer his own question that he has asked of Jesus. Jesus then answers this man's attempt at justifying himself (as being righteous) with the famous parable of the "Good Samaritan." Jesus then clarifies this parable for all of us by the use of a question, followed by an exhortation to apply the lesson of the parable, as answered by this man. Within the Gospels, there are many more examples of Jesus using questions in the process of His teaching. His example reveals the great effectiveness of leading people into the truth through the use of questions.

Learning how to develop Inductive Questions and leading an Inductive Bible Study is a *skill* that requires time and experience to do well. It takes time to develop this skill even if a person has a gift for teaching. A person's skill or ability will be directly related to the time they invest. The more experience gained the better your skill. There really are *no shortcuts*. However, there *are* some ways the process of learning can be greatly benefitted.

Learn by watching others who are more experienced and skilled than you. You can also learn from mistakes, both your own and those you observe as they are learning. Even veterans will make mistakes, get lazy, or have times when they struggle. So, keep learning, and keep looking for ways to develop so you can ask questions in a better way.

Of course, keep asking the Holy Spirit for guidance and grace! It is *not* just some mechanical process to be learned. As with all types of ministry, we all need to be humble, well grounded in the truth of God, open to learning even while teaching, and led by God's Spirit.

```
Now - learn how to Develop Inductive Questions...
```

Developing Inductive Question Skills

Observation Questions

Leading people into *discovering* important details in a text

Reading carefully and repeatedly is always the most important and the first step in observing a text. The more thorough your reading of the text being studied, the more you will observe. The more you observe in your studies, the better you will be able to lead others in observing a text.

Survey Questions

Survey questions use the Key Questions — *Who, What, Where, When, and How* — to guide people in their own observations, and their own examination of a Bible text. Some *general* survey questions are — What is the story about? What are the details of the story? Can you re-tell the story in your own words (IYOW)?

Who are the people involved? *Who* are they related to or involved with? *Who* are they speaking to, interacting with...? **What** are they doing or saying? *What* is the setting of the story, parable, epistle…? *What* is taking place, *What* events or activities are going on? *What* are the people's emotions, reactions, responses...?

When are these events and actions taking place? *When* does the story take place, *When* was this Bible text written? Are there any other *references to time or timing* of events, actions, etc.? **Where** are these people living? *Where* are they coming from, or ...going to? *Where* are these events and actions taking place? Are there any other *references to geography, locations, places*, etc.? **How** are the people acting? ...speaking? *How* are circumstances or events taking place? *How* are people affected by the circumstances and events? Are there any *specific ways of how* things take place mentioned?

Survey Questions are simply questions that help people make accurate observations. In the same way that observation in the inductive study (as with LWS) is the first, most important step of our study approach, this is true of survey questions. They provide a foundation and a frame of reference for people to examine the Bible text, so they can understand its truth. These survey questions lay the groundwork for introducing questions that are more interpretive — questions that cause people to dig deeper into the fertile ground of God's Living Word, the Bible.

Interpretation Questions
Helping people *examine and understand* the truth discovered

Asking the general question "*Why?*" helps people begin thinking about what they have discovered through the use of survey questions. "Why?" is the general question and there are many other ways of asking it. The goal is to examine whatever Scripture text is being studied more thoroughly.

Preschool children are somewhat famous for asking the question, "why?" In fact, they can frazzle a parent (or any person) with their insatiable curiosity. It is because they want to learn about nearly everything they see, hear, experience, or come into their minds. They are looking for meaning, insight, and significance in the world around them. Good interpretation questions can stir a similar childlike curiosity for the truth.

This is the idea behind interpretation questions. These types of questions are simply a way of probing deeper than the surface of what can be observed. It is a way of getting both the *big picture* and *insight* into the smallest of details. But, the big or detailed picture still needs to be seen accurately.

Good (or true) interpretation can only be based on accurate observation. *Why* are these people saying these things, or... doing these things? *Why* are they here or there? *Why* are they here (or there) at this time? *Why* are they speaking this way, or... acting, ...reacting, ...responding, this way, etc.?

"*Why?*" can be asked in *different ways* without really using the word *why*. For example — "What do you think is going on in the minds of the people? How can this be true? Could there be any other reasons the people responded that way? How do you think you might have responded in this situation?"

These and similar questions can be used to stimulate people into thinking more deeply about what they have read and observed. Interpretation questions are a way to apply the basic rules of interpretation (hermeneutics) within the process of an interactive, discussion-based Bible study.

Defining important and key words is also a simple, but important part of the interpretation process of the LWS. The goal is to find out the meaning of these key or important words. We are simply looking more closely at the context of whatever Scripture is being studied.

How is the word used within the text? What is the immediate context (surrounding words and phrases)? How does the rest of the text (larger context) relate to this word, phrase, or idea? The *way* a word is used or expressed within a text is how we should understand its *meaning*. Otherwise, we are taking the word out of its context, or reading another meaning into it.

You can also look for parallel verses within the immediate context or in other places within the Bible that may help give insight. But, be careful about asking for other verses outside of the text you are studying. This could lead to rabbit trails and discussion that is unrelated to the text being studied.

If a dictionary is available, you can ask people to look up specific words. But the definition found in a dictionary may not fit how the same word is used within a certain place. Remember, *the way a word is used* within a given context (Scripture text) is what gives the word or phrase its *meaning.*

There is a more simple way to define words. When looking more closely at certain words in a text, ask people to give definitions in their own words. The acronym, IYOW, can be used when encouraging people to think about what they are reading and studying. This requires them to really think through the meaning of the words in front of them. It gets them processing what may seem obvious or familiar.

Too often, the tendency in defining important words is to use other Scripture verses. But this does not really *define* anything, it simply reiterates or reinforces a word or phrase. Christian terminology is also used often as a means of *defining* words or phrases, but this is simply more reiteration of the same. Many a teacher has told their students, "you can't define a word by using the word itself." The same principle applies here.

Putting words and phrases in a Bible text in our own words is *not* quite as simple as it may seem. It can be both challenging and enlightening. I (the author) have watched people, including pastors, struggle in trying to express the truth of God's Word in their own, thought-out words. Yet, I have seen people really grow in their understanding of the truth when they have accepted the challenge of putting things *IYOW.*

Are there any figures of speech or words used differently than their usual way? This is another important part of defining words within a text. The Bible is *full* of figurative language. (Actually, the previous statement is figurative itself!) The simple goal of defining figurative language is understanding the purpose for it used by the person speaking or writing it. This can be challenging, but again, *the immediate and general context is very important.*

Speaking of the general context, here are some questions to consider. "How do the customs and traditions of that time affect what is said in the text? How were historical circumstances or geographical conditions affecting the people, this situation? How are they important to the story?"

Understanding these things will often require outside sources from the text you are studying. Again, use caution here so as not to introduce ideas that were not intended by the author. So, go to the *original* author, God.

Ask the Holy Spirit to guide you in this process.

```
Now - learn how to use inductive questions for
application in life…
```

Application Questions
Challenging people to *practice* what has been learned

Challenge people to put the truth into life action. "Is this truth alive in my life now? *What* needs to change in my daily life? *How* does my attitude need to change in response to what I have learned? *How* does what I've learned affect my relationship with God? Or, my relationship with others?"

Exhort people to consider specific ways of applying the truth. "*How* can this truth become alive and active in my life? *What* are some *specific ways* it can become active and alive in me? *When* will I *begin* to make these changes? *How* will I begin doing it?"

Application is typically the most difficult of the three basic steps of the inductive-based study. This is also true of developing inductive application questions that challenge, exhort, and encourage people to put the truth they have discovered into life action. These questions need to be specific, yet asked in tactful and gracious ways.

Developing Inductive Study Questions

There is a lot more to actually leading small groups using inductive questions. There are various dynamics to leading a small group that needs to be considered along with the instruction given here. Below are some websites (URLs) you can look at that should help provide additional guidance on leading small groups. There are many books on the subject available in Christian bookstores online.

Some Resources for Leading Small Groups

www.christianitytoday.com/smallgroups

www.ccnonline.net/ccn/smallgroups.htm

www.churchteams.com

www.smallgroups.com

www.smallgroupfriends.com

www.smallgrouphelp.com

```
Now - see how to prepare for leading a Bible
study using Inductive Questions...
```

Preparing for an Inductive Question Bible Study

1. **Start with *your own* thorough inductive study of the text you will be teaching.** *All* questions need to be based on *your own* completed study of the text. Make sure *you* understand what you will be asking others to learn. Help lead people to discover what you have discovered in your own study.

2. ***Review* your outline and (LWS) notebook charting of the text.** Note where segments of the text begin and end (as with a simple outline learned in LWS). Develop questions segment by segment. Mark specific things in your own notebook study that you can base questions upon.

3. **Remember to work from what has *personally* ministered to *you*.** Always begin with what has become *life* to you. *What is alive and active in your heart?* Put another way, how can you lead others into discovering the truth, *if you have not already done so*?

4. ***Always* begin with Observation questions.** As you study a *segment* of text, build a foundation for understanding with survey questions, using the Key Questions. Your questions should help people see the relationship between the details observed in the Scripture text.

5. **Introduce Interpretation Questions — *based* on what's been observed.** As a foundation is built, help people reflect on and consider what has been discovered. Interpretation questions should lead people into a deeper and fuller understanding of the truth in the text.

6. **Make a *few* good Application Questions when useful.** Usually, only one (1) application question is needed per segment of text. One good application question, after other questions have made the truth clear and real, can be very powerful. One well-developed and asked application question is far more effective than several weak application questions.

7. **Put your Questions in the Order you need to Ask them.** One question should lead into the next as if walking up a set of stairs. Observation questions lead up to Interpretation questions. An application question (or two) is based on what has been observed and understood up to that point. The application question would be like a landing on a set of stairs, a place to reflect upon what has been learned. There should be *a group of questions* for *each segment* of the text being studied.

8. **Review your questions and the order you will be asking them.** Are your questions developed on the guidelines above and the previous instruction? Do they match the goals as outlined on the next page?!

Goals of an Inductive Question Bible Study

1. **All your questions must be *answerable* from the *text*.** Will people be *able* to answer your questions based on reading and reflecting upon the text? Can *you* answer all your own questions?! If *not*, then *don't* ask these questions of others!

2. **Make sure your questions are *simple and clear*.** Will people understand what you are asking for? *Don't* try to make your questions difficult! You *want* people to discover the truth! You may need follow-up questions to your initial question.

3. **Make sure your questions are really *observing, interpreting or applying* the text studied.** As you form your questions, ask yourself the following questions — "Can they be answered from *your* inductive study? Is your wording clear and direct, as you ask them to observe, interpret or apply the truth?"

4. **Questions should *flow* from one question to the next, throughout the study.** Do your questions *lead* a person through the text naturally and smoothly? There needs to be a logical connection between one question and the next one.

5. **When asking your questions, *allow* people to *discover* the truth on their own.** Let people have enough time to answer the questions. *Don't* answer them yourself! When people are having difficulty answering the question, encourage them to return to the text often. *"Look at the text, what does it say?"* Or, another way of putting this, *"Is that what you see in the text? Is that in agreement with what we learned so far?"*

6. **Discussion, based on the questions and the text, needs to be *fruitful and edifying*.** *Don't* shame people when they answer incorrectly! Encourage them to keep trying! *Don't* let other peoples' answers or discussions get the discussion off track and confuse others. Simply ask them, *"Is that what the text tells us? Does that agree with what we've already learned?"* While leading discussions, you need to be helping people discover the truth within

Developing Inductive Study Questions

the text. You are simply the guide. You're leading them because *you've gone there before them* with your own inductive study of the text, your own discovery of truth.

7. **An inductive question-based Bible study should lead to a *practical understanding* of the text.** The value of observation questions is helping people carefully examine and discover the truth in a Scripture text. The purpose of interpretation questions is to help people gain a clear understanding of the truth discovered. The goal of application questions is to guide people into putting the truth into action in their own lives. An application needs to be *personal* and *practical*!

See the following examples for how to draw from your inductive study notebook to develop inductive questions for each step of the inductive study process.

1. The first step is to develop some survey questions from your observations of the text (see pages 58-59)

2. In the second step, review the interpretation insights of your inductive study of the text (see pages 60-61)

3. Then, form questions to help people to see how they can make an application of the truth of the text as you review how you realized how to apply the truth of the text for yourself. (see pages 62-63)

4. Finally, put your inductive questions in a sequence that leads people through the text based on the previous guidance and example on pages 65 and 66. See the exercise for you to complete on page 67.

Developing Inductive Study Questions

Observations (Obs)
LWS Notebook — inductive study work

John 13:1-5 — 1st Segment — *Jesus begins washing the disciples' feet*

vs 1 —
- before the feast of the Passover
- Jesus
- knew the hour had come
- He should depart from this world
- (go) to the Father
- having loved His own
- He loved them to the end

vs 2 —
- supper being ended
- the devil
- having already put it into the heart of Judas
- to betray Him

vs 3 —
- Jesus knowing that the Father had given all things into His hands
- that He had come from God
- was going to God

vs 4 —

  (your own work here...)

vs 5 —

  (your own work here...)

Examples of inductive Observation (Survey) questions
(based on observations from your inductive study work)

Inductive Questions

- (Obs) *Can you tell this story in your own words?*
- (Obs) *What specific things did Jesus know in verses 1-3?*
- (Obs) *What specific actions did Jesus take in verses 1-5?*
- (Obs) *Who are other people involved in or mentioned in this segment?*

Now— write your own Observation questions below—

- **Exercise #1 –**
  - **Develop your own Observation questions**
  - **Either, ask similar questions, but in your own words, or make your own — make sure they match the goals of an inductive question Bible study!**

Interpretations (Int)

LWS Notebook — inductive study work

John 13:1-5 — 1st Segment — *Jesus begins washing the disciples' feet*

vs 1 —

(Passover) an annual feast Jewish men are required to attend in Jerusalem as a memorial of God's deliverance from Egypt (Exodus 12)

(Jesus) is Lord, Messiah, God coming as man upon the earth— the One who had come as "the Lamb of God" to take away the sin of the world (Jn 1:29). Jesus knew it was time for Him to fulfill His work of redemption upon the Cross and return to the Father in Heaven

Jesus had demonstrated His love to the disciples and people of Israel many times by showing them mercy, teaching, praying for them and healing them— now He would be showing the great depth of His love upon the Cross for His disciples, Israel and all mankind

(vs 2)

The Passover meal He was sharing with the disciples (Lk 22:15). The enemy of God (devil) and believers, the Adversary, Satan. Because of Judas's bitterness and greed, his heart was open to the prompting of Satan (Jn 12:4-6). Judas (1 of "the 12") would betray Jesus to the Jewish authorities (Sanhedrin) for 30 pieces of silver (Mt 26:14-16)

(vs 3)

Jesus knew all authority had been given to Him by His Father even before this time. He knew the purpose for which He was sent to the earth as "the Lamb of God", the Only Son of God. He knew He would be returning to His place at the right hand of the Father after His resurrection from the dead

(vss 4 & 5)

(your own work here)

Examples of inductive Interpretation questions
(based on interpretation insights from your inductive study work)

Inductive Questions

(Int) **Why *do you think the apostle John makes it clear what Jesus knew?***

(Int) **Why *is this important or necessary?***

(Int) **How *does what Jesus knew relate to His washing the disciples' feet?***

(Int) **How *does Jesus "love them to the end" and how is this related to His washing their feet?***

Now— write your own Interpretation questions below—

- Exercise #2 –
    - **Develop your own Interpretation questions**
    - **Either, ask similar questions, but in your own words, or make your own — make sure they match the goals of an inductive question Bible study!**

Application (App)
LWS Notebook — inductive study work

John 13:1-5 — 1st Segment — *Jesus begins washing the disciples' feet*

"WHAT" —

Even as Jesus demonstrated His love for the disciples, I also need to consider ways in which I can love others beyond whatever ways I demonstrate love to them now.

I especially need to think about those I find it hard to love or express love towards... *(you fill in your answer)*

I need to... *(you fill in your answer)*

"HOW" —

I need to consider the practical ways Jesus showed love to other people throughout the Gospels, as well as to His disciples.

I can actually love others in these ways... *(give some actual and practical ways of showing love to specific people)*

I will ... *(you fill in your answer)*

Examples of inductive Application questions
(based on observations and insights from your inductive study work)

Inductive Questions

- (App) What *practical truth can you apply in your own life from what we have learned? (be specific!)*
- (App) What *are ways others have served you?*
- (App) What *are ways in which you have humbled yourself as a servant of others?*
- (App) What *are specific ways you are serving others now?*
- (App) How *would you accept someone of greater authority or position serving you, as Jesus did with His disciples?*
- (App) How *can you put this practical truth into action in your own life? (be specific!)*

Now— write your own Application questions below—

- Exercise #3 –
  - **Develop your own Interpretation questions**
  - **Either, ask similar questions, but in your own words, or make your own — make sure they match the goals of an inductive question Bible study!**

Developing Inductive Study Questions

Example of Using Inductive Questions in a Study Setting

1. **Pray!** *And maybe have a time of praise and worship!*
2. **Give people a general idea** of how much of the text you want to study at this time
3. **After reading the text** — *usually a section, but **no less than a segment***
   a. *This will help give a **frame of reference** and context for the inductive questions*
   b. *When leading an ongoing study with a group of people — have them read the whole text **before** coming to the study*
4. **Begin with your Inductive Questions** — using your question to lead the people through the text.

> See the example on the next page of a set of inductive questions for the text of John 13:1-5.
>
> Notice the sequence of Observation (Obs), Interpretation (Int), and Application (App) questions.
>
> Each question should lead to the next, just as the questions that follow them move forward on the foundation of the previous questions with the application questions at the end.

An example of a set of Inductive Questions for John 13:1-5

(Obs) *Can you (anyone in the group) tell this story in your own words?*

(Obs) *What specific things did Jesus know in verses 1-3?*

(Obs) *Who are other people involved or mentioned in this segment?*

(Int) *Why do you think the apostle John makes it clear what Jesus knew?*

(Obs) *What are the specific times mentioned in this segment?*

(Int) *Why are these "times" important and how do they relate to one another?*

(Int) *How can we know what it means by, "His hour had come"?*

(Obs) *What specific actions does Jesus take in these few verses (1-5)?*

(Int) *How does Jesus "love them to the end" and how is this related to His washing their feet?*

(App) *What are ways others have served you?*

(App) *What are ways in which you have humbled yourself as a servant of others?*

(App) *How are you are serving others now? (be specific!)*

- Exercise #4 –

As a completion of the work using the Living Word Study workbook — Develop Inductive Questions for all of John 13:1-17, following the instructions and examples given above and before this page — *work directly from your own charting and the text of John 13:1-17.*

Continue through the text — *segment by segment.* Develop a group of Inductive Questions for each segment.

Simply follow the example above and the instructions before this page. Notice how one question leads to the next, and how the different types of questions — *observation, interpretation, and application* — are woven together leading to the application questions at the end. It may be helpful to have follow-up questions to clarify what you are asking for or to expand on the initial question.

```
    See the following pages for more insight into the
learning process of using Inductive Questions for
leading people through a Bible text for a fuller, deeper
understanding of the truth in God's Living Word.
```

Developing Inductive Study Questions

Understanding the learning process when using Inductive Questions

A vivid memory...

As a young boy, I grew up along the coast of Southern California during the 1950s and '60s. I remember playing on the bluffs overlooking the state beach in the town where I lived. Back then it was not developed, nor particularly safe according to today's standards. But it was a great place to play, imagine and grow up!

At that time, there were some houses built along the beach and on the cliffs above the beach. These were owned by people who had either been in the area a long time or who were wealthy. In most cases, they were pretty wealthy. We had family friends who built a house on these bluffs that were actually fairly steep cliffs. They had a staircase built from the top of the bluff, where their house was built, to the bottom, where the beach was.

I remember the first time up and down those stairs — it was a long way, either way! Every so often there were landings, and the stairs actually switch-backed across the bluff in some places. There were also a couple of gates in the lower section and at the top for security. I can remember climbing up those stairs with some fear and trembling since I had a fear of heights. But I remember how great it was to climb up and view the Pacific Ocean and the beach below at various levels along the way.

This is still a vivid picture in my mind to this day. I have visited the same house, and stairs, and an added beach house with my family over the past few decades. It's still beautiful, and it is a great illustration of the idea of leading people through a Bible study using inductive questions. It isn't a straight line, but it *is* a solid pathway to and from the beach that has stood the test of time. The reason it has stood all these years? It is built upon the rock at the core of the bluffs, not upon sand. Living Word Study, the inductive study approach, is grounded upon God's Word. (See Matthew 7:24)

The learning process...

Observation is the first and most important step of the inductive study process (as with LWS) — it is the foundation.

Actually, God's Word, the Bible text, is the foundation. But observation questions are built upon the foundation of the Bible text and need to be the beginning point for an effective inductive question-led study. Just as a set of stairs need to be set on a firm footing (the foundation). Even the risers and landings need to be anchored upon footings. The long, seemingly vertical staircase on the bluff was supported by posts that went down to footings dug deep into the bedrock of the bluff.

An inductive question-led study is a *process* of discovery. Observation and survey questions provide the beginning point for the study to be developed. So, the questions need to help people continue referring to the text for a complete, accurate examination of the Scripture being studied. Too often, important details are missed because of careless reading or impatience to delve deeper into the text.

Observation and survey questions are not just the beginning, they provide the basis for a further, deeper examination of the truth in a text. As taught in LWS, reading, and rereading are essential to good, accurate observation. When people are given the opportunity and challenge to retell the story in their own words or to restate the text in their own words, the transition to interpretation begins.

Inductive questions are introduced after a good foundation is laid through observation and survey questions.

As important details are discovered and seen more clearly, as their relationship and connection to one another is understood, interpretation questions can be asked. Using interpretation questions, people are asked to look deeper into the text — not only to look for meaning, but attitudes, motives, intents, and reasons.

When people are challenged to think about what they have observed and discovered, they begin processing truth at a deeper level. Not just mentally (cognitively), but spiritually. This makes it possible for them to internalize the truth, in a sense, *making it their own.* Of course, the truth of the Bible has always been there, but as they discover and understand it, it becomes a part of them (internally).

The more this process continues—*discovering by observation, digging deeper with interpretation questions*—there is often an internal struggle going on. This grappling and wrestling with the truth enables people to grasp the truth at a deeper level—*both mentally and spiritually*—and gain a deeper understanding of it. This is often an exponential process, since the Holy Spirit will reveal further depth of the truth in connection to other Biblical truth. As the truth begins working within a person, they should begin seeing how it is *personally* related to their life.

Back to the staircase. I can remember climbing up those stairs, every once and a while stopping to look around. I didn't really like looking straight down, nor was it very encouraging to look up at the distance I still needed to climb. But I recall taking stock of the view I had at various levels. I was also reminded of how small I was in comparison to all that was around me — the bluff, the beach, and the vast Pacific Ocean. Somehow, I realized how blessed I was, how privileged I was to have this access to and from this house and beach. It was and still is a precious memory. On those same bluffs I spent many an evening gazing out over the ocean, watching a sunset, and contemplating life in general. In later years, I came to discover my own place within God's Kingdom and was baptized in a nearby cove that was walking distance from that set of stairs I had climbed as a boy.

Application questions should naturally follow interpretation questions.

As this learning process continues, it needs some type of resolution or completion. This is where application comes in. Application questions should challenge and encourage people to put the truth understood into life action. Application questions need to be built upon a solid foundation and understanding of the truth discovered. If a study goes no further than the process of thinking, as in the interpretation process, all that is understood will *not* benefit a person. It simply becomes more knowledge gained and perhaps stored, but it will *not* become *life*.

Jesus makes this clear in John 15. There, Jesus uses the analogy of being the true Vine and His followers being branches. There is only one purpose for the branch of a grapevine, it is to produce grapes — *fruit*! This was the primary point of His instruction about "abiding in Him", that we believers would "bear much fruit", and that His words would "abide" in us as we "abide" in Him. There needs to be a *natural and useful product* of our study in His Word.

Often, the problem is not, "What do I need to do?" — *or* — "What should I do?" This may not be so difficult to discover. The more difficult thing is knowing *how* to do something, *in what way*, or even *when*. So, good application questions need to be *specific, personal, and practical*. The truth needs to become *useful* in our lives, not just as spiritual knowledge, concepts, or theories. After people have discovered and processed the truth of a text, they need to be led on to a practical, personal application of the truth for their own lives.

This takes some reflection on the part of people. Here is where the idea of the landing on a staircase comes to my mind. Observation and interpretation questions need to be developed and designed to lead to a clear application of the truth. As I walked up those flights of stairs, it was not always a good idea to stop on an individual step to look around. These stairs went up a cliff! If not careful, I could lose my balance as I became so absorbed in what I was looking out at. The landing at the top of each flight of stairs provided a good, stable platform to look around and take stock of my surroundings. But remember, I had to climb many steps to get to those landings along the way.

Another memory about stairs...

My family and I moved to the Philippines in 1990. For many years we lived on a beautiful, mountainous island. We still oversee and maintain a ministry there. As a family and when visitors came, we liked to hike up into the mountains behind our city, then down into a canyon on a set of "stairs" or steps carved into the canyon wall. Then we made our way up the canyon, along the river, to a magnificent waterfall that poured into a nice pool of cool water. The Philippines is in a tropical setting, it gets very hot and humid, and this was a very refreshing place.

The place is called Casa Roro, which basically means "house of the roar." The waterfall is somewhere around 80 to 100 feet high, coming out of sheer, unclimbable cliffs, so it is quite loud. This area is one of the last places on our island where you can see remnants of the tropical rainforest that covered the island long ago. The path to and from the falls is long and hard. By the time we would get to the falls, we were sweaty, dusty and ready to swim! Going back out and up was equally as hard, and we got equally dusty and sweaty on the way back. *What's the point?* Leading people in an inductive question-led study can be a lot of work, even frustrating at times. But it *is* worth the effort. Everyone we ever brought to Casa Roro agreed, "this is incredibly beautiful and worth the hike!" *Get the picture?!*

This is the cover of a study devotional published in September 2020. It's available online at– https://tripkimball.com/shop
Or on Amazon– Stories of Redemption

STORIES
OF REDEMPTION

A DEVOTIONAL JOURNEY
THROUGH THE BOOK OF RUTH

TRIP KIMBALL

An Inductive Study of the Book of Ruth

Copyright Info

The material in this booklet was originally protected under copyright issued on November 12, 1999, in the Republic of the Philippines — Registration No. A 99-1238

Permission to copy and distribute the Study Guide needs to be requested from the author—

Pastor Trip Kimball
Jacksonville Beach, FL 32250, USA
E-mail – info@word-strong.com

Cover artwork ©2020 Laura Williams

How to utilize the Study Questions and Background information

The study questions (for each chapter) are designed to help you read and think about what you're reading and studying within the text itself.

The Book of Ruth is not a random romantic story, but a significant look at the sovereignty of God and His plan of redemption for all people within the world. It contains interesting character studies of the main people—Naomi, Ruth and Boaz. Read through the contextual notes provided before the study questions.

The Mosaic Law and history of Israel give prophetic insight to make the history of the Bible relevant to our own time. Ruth provides a sort of *God's-eye view* into the history of Israel and the world.

Keep a notebook handy to write down important things you learn as you read and study. Use the Living Word Study–Journal Notebook for your IBS study notes and answers to the study questions for each chapter (see explanation on pages 27-29 and sample on last page of Addenda).

The study questions are designed to walk you through the story so you can observe and interpret what you read in the text, and apply truth clarified through the study process.

Put yourself in the story when studying Narratives and use your imagination to identify with the people involved. There are four important things to note when studying Narratives—people, places, events and actions, and time.

An Inductive Study of the Book of Ruth

BACKGROUND AND CONTEXTUAL NOTES
ON THE BOOK OF RUTH

The Book of Ruth is a Narrative—a story. The value and purpose for studying Ruth and other Narratives is learning from the examples of people within the story along with revealed truth in the story.

We are given insight into God's relationships and interaction with people along with a view of their character. We are able to see their values, beliefs, struggles, and other responses towards God, various events, other people, and situations in their lives and whatever else may unfold in the story.

There are four important elements to take note of while studying Narratives (things that have significance). People, obviously, play an important role in stories. Not only the people themselves, but their roles in the story, their heritage and origins, their culture, manners, and customs. Places, where the story takes place. The geographic locations and regions, travel and distances, the environment people are in and the physical locations that are part of the landscape, or a house or tent.

Events and actions that take place within the story are what help bring the story to life. This may include the various conversations of people, responses of people (to what takes place in the story), emotions, motives, and many other great or intricate things that may happen in a story. The fourth element is time, which includes when the story takes place in history, the chronological and sequential progress of time, and any other markers of time that involve events and actions.

These four elements often overlap and are interwoven within the story because they are interrelated. In other words, things don't happen in a vacuum or without purpose—people do things in certain places, at certain times, and in certain ways.

An Inductive Study of the Book of Ruth

TIME AND SETTING

The story of Ruth is set during the time of the Judges. The judges were rulers sent by God as deliverers when the people of Israel would cry out to the Lord for help from their oppressors. The time period of their rule was about 335-340 years (see timeline). The time of the rule of these judges was known by much moral and spiritual corruption, followed by enslavement or bondage to other nations, a crying out to the Lord, a deliverer (judge) being sent, and a period of stability and rest.

Over all, it was a time of darkness and turmoil in Israel's history. The story of Ruth stands out in contrast. It is not just the romantic love story of two people but the love story of God's everlasting and gracious love to humanity. It is a story of people who were faithful to the God of Israel.

One of these people is not even Jewish but a Moabitess, a young woman from the neighboring nation of Moab. Moab was located about 80 km (50 mi) from Bethlehem, east of the Dead Sea. The Moabites were descendants of Lot, through his daughters (by incest).

The actual time of this story is hard to fix but might be sometime around 1100 BC. The traditional view has Samuel as the author, but it appears to be written during King David's time because of its literary style and David's name being last in the genealogy in Chapter 4.

The importance of the story is timeless. It gives us a picture of God's plan of redemption long before the Redeemer of all mankind—Jesus Christ who was descended from Boaz and Ruth—comes as the Father's love-gift to the world.

CULTURAL BACKGROUND

There is considerable insight given within the text of the customs and ways of people in those days. This is seen through the relationships of the main characters not only between themselves but also with others. Note those whom Boaz relates to, including Ruth and Naomi, his workers, the nearest kinsman-redeemer, and the elders. The relationship between Naomi and Ruth also provides insight into the status of women in those days, and the relationship of Jews and Gentiles.

Chapter 2, and other places where time is mentioned, give us insight about their customs and ways of harvesting, including the explanation of the finalizing of the redemption in Chapter 4. For more information, see books on Biblical Manners and Customs or Bible Dictionaries.

An important cultural insight related to the main theme of the story and its important theological emphasis is the role of the kinsman-redeemer. Biblical background is given in Leviticus 25:23-28 and Deuteronomy 25:5-10. This portion of the Law deals with redemption of property and the continuing of a family line.

The genealogy in Chapter 4 is also important because it shows the family line of Boaz traced back to Perez, the son of Judah, which is another story of continuing a family line. This is especially important because it is the family line of King David, but more importantly—the family line of the most important Kinsman-Redeemer, Jesus Christ, who was also born in Bethlehem.

An Inductive Study of the Book of Ruth

THEOLOGICAL INSIGHTS AND TERMS

- **Genealogy**— the record of ancestors for a family line—especially important to Israel because all Israel was descended from the patriarch Abraham. His descendants were heirs of the covenant between Abraham and God, which includes the expected Messiah through the line of David, the tribe of Judah.

- **Kinsman-Redeemer**— in Hebrew—*goel*—can mean to free or redeem (by repayment), and redemption or freedom—either the act of redemption or the redeemer himself. These are the requirements for a kinsman-redeemer—he must be a blood-relative, directly related, have the means (monies) to purchase (redeem) the property, be willing to purchase the forfeited land or inheritance, be willing to marry the wife of the deceased kinsman—Mahlon or Kilion, the sons of Elimelech.

- **Redemption**— buying back what was sold or given at some point. The idea is an important part of the Year of Jubilee (Leviticus 25) and other areas of the Law. Redemption is also what we call the work of Christ upon the Cross who bought back (redeemed) humanity from sin with the price of His life.

- **Providence of God**— how God sovereignly directs and provides for His people (believers) through circumstances and timely events. An example is Naomi's family moving to Moab because of famine, her son marrying Ruth, Ruth going to work in Boaz's field, Boaz's redemption of Elimelech's property and marrying Ruth.

- **Sovereignty of God**— God's omnipotent authority, power, and rule over all. We see God's divine plan for man's redemption from sin first expressed in Genesis 3:15, further expressed in Ruth through the divine providence of Ruth working in Boaz's field, where Obed becomes part of the Messianic line that later brings salvation to Gentiles (Matt 1:5-6).

PEOPLE IN RUTH

The meaning and significance of their Names

- **Ruth**— *friendship*—an indication of her faithfulness and loyalty of character
- **Boaz**— *in Him is strength*—a man of standing and strong moral character
- **Naomi**— *pleasant one*—after many difficulties she wants her name to be changed to Mara—*bitter*—but in the end is blessed and restored
- **Elimelech**— *God is my king*—during the time of the judges, God was to be the only king of Israel
- **Mahlon**— *sick or weakling*—he dies after 10 years in Moab
- **Kilion**— *pining or finished*—after his death Naomi hears of better times in Bethlehem and leaves Moab
- **Orpah**— *neck or stubbornness*—unlike Ruth, she returns to her own people and gods
- **Bethlehem**— *house of bread*—a place of provision for Naomi and Ruth, also the birthplace of Jesus—the *Bread of Life*

TYPES

Typology is when something (or someone) prophetically represents another more important thing or person coming in the future—an illustration. "Ruth" has several Types or Typical elements that are fulfilled in the New Testament.

- Boaz— the kinsman-redeemer in the line of David is a picture (Type) of Christ who would come as the Redeemer for all humanity and his character, like Christ's, reflects virtue, integrity, honesty, loyalty, responsibility, and humility. The word *goel* (kinsman-redeemer) is mentioned 13 times in Ruth

- Ruth— the Moabitess (a Gentile) becomes the bride of Boaz and brings her into the line of David and Christ the Messiah. Her character reflects Christ's nature with her virtue, honesty, loyalty, responsibility, and humility. She is one of four women mentioned in the genealogy of Matthew 1 and one of two Gentiles. She is a picture (type) of the Gentiles brought into God's promise of inheritance through Christ's redemption

- Naomi— mother in law to Ruth—could represent Israel (as a type)—Israel was called to be a *light unto the Gentiles.* Naomi is the door (entry point) for Ruth's inclusion into the Messianic line

- Redemption of Elimelech's property— a picture of Christ's redemption upon the Cross since man cannot redeem himself, he needs another Kinsman-Redeemer (1 Cor. 15:21-22, 45-50)

TIME LINE FOR THE BOOK OF RUTH

The time and setting of the Book of Ruth can only be estimated in recorded history. The first Judge of Israel, as recorded in the Bible, is Othniel (beginning about 1380-1375 BC). The next to last one is Samson whose death is about 1050-45 BC. Samuel is considered both a Judge and Prophet of Israel—a *spiritual bridge* between the times of the Judges and the Kings.

> [BC = *Before Christ*—time progresses with dates decreasing / AD = *In the Year of our Lord*—dates increase]

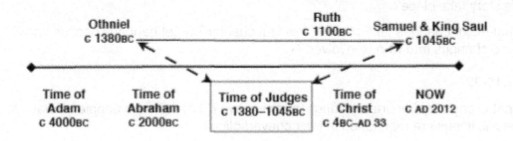

Dates based on various references from Study Bibles and the Book of Judges

An Inductive Study of the Book of Ruth

Ruth Study Questions
A guide for reading and studying
Chapter 1

Chapter 1:1-14—

1. How does the story begin? Can you retell it in your own words?
2. When does this story take place and what significant event takes place at the beginning?
3. Who are the people mentioned here and what is said about them? Where does this story take place?
4. What major changes take place in this first chapter? What happens because of these changes and who is involved?

Chapter 1:15-22—

1. What is one very important change involving two (2) of the main people? What specific things are mentioned in their conversation?
2. Who does most of the talking and what is the result? What stands out to you about Ruth's statements?
3. What things take place at the end of this chapter? How is the end of the chapter different than the beginning? Do you see any type of resolve or completion within Chapter 1?
4. Could this be an applicable truth for you and your life? Has the Lord spoken to you personally about how you need to trust in Him?

An Inductive Study of the Book of Ruth

Ruth Study Questions
A guide for reading and studying
Chapter 2

Chapter 2:1-16—
1. What important information is given about a certain man? How is this man described?
2. What request does Ruth make of Naomi and what is Naomi's response?
3. What takes place according to Ruth's request and action? Do you think this is by chance? If not, who's plan is it, Naomi's or the Lord's?
4. How does Boaz greet his workers and what do they tell him about Ruth? How does the conversation between Boaz and Ruth begin? What does Boaz tell Ruth and what is her response to him (in verses 7-10)?
5. What other things do Boaz and Ruth say to one another? How does he treat her? Would this be expected, or is it unusual for that time?
6. What else does Boaz say to his workers (young men) about Ruth? Do you think he is extending special favor to her, or is this typical and expected? What does this tell you about Boaz as a man?

Chapter 2:17-23—
1. At the end of the day, how much has Ruth gleaned and gathered?
2. What is Naomi's response to Ruth when she returns? How does Naomi respond to Ruth once she knows whose field she worked in?
3. How is what Naomi says in verse 20 different from what she says in Chap 1:20-21? What has changed? Why is this important to the story?
4. What is Naomi's further advice to Ruth? How does she respond to Naomi's advice? How long does she stay with the young women of Boaz?
5. Do you see anything in this chapter relevant for your own life? How has God called you to be faithful in whatever work or service you do?

An Inductive Study of the Book of Ruth

Ruth Study Questions
A guide for reading and studying
Chapter 3

Chapter 3:1-9—
1. What does Naomi want to do for Ruth? What does she tell Ruth to do? What does it sound like Naomi is trying to do?
2. Do you think this is a good thing, a manipulative plan, or the Lord's direction? What is Ruth's response to Naomi?
3. What does Ruth actually do when she goes to the threshing floor? When does this happen? Does this seem right to you, or do you think it was culturally appropriate for those days?
4. What is Boaz's response when he discovers Ruth? What happens next? What request does Ruth make of Boaz? Is this what Naomi told her to do or is it culturally proper?

Chapter 3:10-18—
1. What actually takes place between Boaz and Ruth (as told in the text)? What does this tell you about their character? What does Boaz say that confirms this?
2. What important commitment does Boaz make to Ruth? What is the actual situation regarding his relationship to Ruth's family? Why is this important?
3. What takes place that night after Boaz declares his intentions and commitment? What does Boaz do to indicate his intentions to Naomi?
4. What does Ruth tell Naomi when Ruth returns in the morning? What is Naomi's response to Ruth when she hears what Boaz says, does, and is planning to do?
5. Do you think all of this is because of Naomi's plan or God's? Why do you think this (either way)? What lesson can you apply in your own life from Chapter 3?

Ruth Study Questions
A guide for reading and studying
Chapter 4

Chapter 4:1-12—

1. What does Boaz do the next day? *In your own words*—How is this event described? How does Boaz present the situation to this other "close relative" (kinsman redeemer)?

2. Do you think Boaz might be manipulating the situation or would this be the usual way of presenting it?

3. Why does Boaz need to offer the land to this other man? Why does the man refuse purchase of this land after saying he wants it?

4. How does he show his refusal? Why is this done? (You may need to refer to Deut. 25:5-10)

5. What does Boaz do and say when the man will not buy the land? Who does he speak to? How do the men respond to Boaz about this? Who else hears Boaz's commitment and what do they say?

6. What things stand out to you about the people's blessings upon Boaz in verses 11-12? Why would verse 12 be significant?

Chapter 4:13-22—

1. What takes place as the story concludes, in verses 13-17? How does the story shift back to Naomi?

2. What is said to Naomi? Who speaks to her and what form does it seem to be given? What is the significance of what these women say to Naomi and about Obed?

3. How is this related to the genealogy at the end? Why would this be important to Israel and their history, especially when this was written?

4. How does the story end for Naomi? How does this compare to the beginning of the story?

5. What simple application can be made from this story as a whole? Do you see any more personal applications for your own life?

If you'd like a study journal set up for inductive study, be sure to see my Living Word Study Journal available on my website— Living Word Study Journal
And on Amazon— Living Word Study Journal

LIVING WORD STUDY JOURNAL
A JOURNAL & NOTEBOOK FOR BIBLE STUDY

For more LWS Inductive Bible Studies
and Resources visit—

https://tripkimball.com/downloads

Made in the USA
Columbia, SC
22 November 2024